Designing the Art of Social Media for Artists

Table of Contents

Art doesn't transform. It just plain forms.

Chapter 1. Introduction

In an ever-evolving digital world, mastering the art of social media has become an imperative skill for artists worldwide. This Special Report, "Designing the Art of Social Media for Artists," promises to guide you through the fascinating labyrinth of hashtags, posts, and likes, to effectively curate your online persona and exhibit your artwork. Crafted with a friendly and vibrant tone, this report candidly decodes the world of social media, translating confusing algorithms into understandable strategies. It's brimming with expert advice, innovative strategies, and real-life success stories to inspire you and turn your artistic journey into a beautiful shared experience. If you're an artist looking to navigate the digital sphere or a creative soul yearning for a spotlight in the virtual art gallery, this endearing report is your treasure-map to claim your rightful space! Unleash your creativity and let's paint the social media canvas in hues of your artistry together. Roll up your sleeves, artists—it's time to make social media your masterpiece!

Chapter 2. Understanding the Social Media Landscape

In the expansive universe of the digital age, a fledgling artist may feel initially overwhelmed by the diversity of social media platforms, each distinctively uniquely in its offering. The first step toward getting comfortable here is to understand that these platforms are nothing more than vast networks of communication, each with its own population, culture, and language.

2.1. Getting acquainted with the major platforms

Facebook, Twitter, Instagram, LinkedIn, Pinterest, Snapchat, TikTok—these names are likely already familiar, being the reigning lords of the social media realm. However, beyond their ubiquity and pop-culture prominence each of these platforms target specific demographics, and house different forms of content. Recognizing the personality of each platform will enable you to better customize your artistic presence.

Facebook, for example, is like the living room of social media, with a diverse and general audience spanning all ages. It primarily thrives on discussion-based posts, making it a great space for direct interaction with your audience through reaffirming posts, elaborate captions, live chats, and more.

Twitter, on the other hand, is essentially the social media newsroom. It's a place for quick updates and sharp discussion, for voicing opinions or sharing ideas in bite-sized inputs. This makes it ideal for audience interactions, real-time commentary, and sharing information related to your artwork or events.

Instagram is an artist's paradise, given its visual-centered nature. People flock here in search of aesthetic inspiration, making it the perfect platform for showcasing your artwork, behind-the-scenes glimpses, and other visually engaging content.

Similarly, the likes of **LinkedIn**, **Pinterest**, **Snapchat**, and **TikTok** each serve their own demographic segments with unique content structures, whether it's professional networking, photo collages, ephemeral content, or short videos.

2.2. Knowing your audience

Understanding social media is not solely about comprehending the platforms. It also entails an in-depth understanding of the people who breathe life into these platforms—the audience.

Here, an essential concept is the 'target audience'. This refers to a specific group of people within the broader audience that you aim to reach with your art. They could be categorized based on their age, location, interests, or any number of demographic, geographic, and psychographic factors. Identifying your target audience involves understanding what they like, the platforms they frequent, and the times when they are most active. Market research tools, peer studies, and audience insights from existing social media platforms can prove invaluable in this endeavor.

2.3. Mapping the competition

While your art is unique, you aren't alone in offering it to the world. You need to know your competitors—other artists vying for the same audience's attention. Through competitor analysis, you can study their social media marketing strategies, understand what works and what doesn't, and incorporate these insights into your own social media strategy. Observing their follower engagement, post frequency, and content strategy can provide valuable lessons in what to do and what not to do.

2.4. Understanding platform algorithms

No understanding of the social media landscape is complete without a grasp of the mystifying algorithms that dictate it. Though these intricate formulas are constantly evolving, knowing the basics can give you a competitive edge.

For instance, most platforms prioritize engagement. That means more likes, comments, shares, or saves your posts receive, the more they're promoted by the platform's algorithm. Understanding this can help you create compelling content designed to provoke interaction from your followers.

2.5. Embracing the trends

Just as art trends evolve, so too does the social media landscape. This dynamism demands that artists stay up to date with the latest trends. Following social media news, attending webinars, and subscribing to dedicated newsletters can keep you in the loop. Whether it's Instagram's shift to IGTV, Facebook's embrace of live video, or Twitter's adoption of Spaces, being in sync with the platform's new features gives your artistic presence a contemporary feel, attracting a tech-savvy audience.

In conclusion, understanding the social media landscape is like learning the rules of an exciting but complex game. The platforms are your arenas, your audience forms the rules of engagement, and exceptionally, your art is the unique game strategy, ready to conquer the digital realm. Comprehend the rhythm of these dynamics, and you've taken your first steps towards mastering the art of social media.

Chapter 3. The Artist's Presence: Crafting Your Online Persona

Creating an impactful online persona is a strategic endeavor where everything from your profile picture to the topics of your posts becomes instrumental in crafting a cohesive, relatable, and unique identity. This 'cyber persona' serves as your virtual alter-ego, a digitized representative of your real-world self, artistry, interests, and ideals.

3.1. Defining Your Artistry

The first step in crafting your online persona is defining your artistry. In the physical world, one's artistic identity is showcased by their exhibits, their style, and the themes encapsulated in their work. In the digital sphere, this needs to be effectively translated to words, images, videos, and even emoticons. Understanding your art is central to projecting your persona. Reflect upon your art; think where does it come from? What does it represent? What does it mean to you? What emotions or reactions does it evoke from others?

3.2. Establishing a Unique Name and Image

Your name and profile picture serve as the primary anchors of your online persona. They're the first things people see while visiting your social media profiles. Your 'internet alias' should ideally be a blend of unique, memorable, and reflective of your artistry. The same applies to your profile picture. This could be a picture of yourself, a logo, or an artistic representation. Settle for an image that presents you or your work in the best light and stimulates intrigue and interest.

3.3. Developing a Consistent Voice

The voice of your posts is the tone and style of your textual communication. This could be professional, casual, witty, or a mix. It's essential to maintain consistency in your voice across platforms to reinforce your persona and build familiarity among your followers. This voice should ideally represent your personality and artistic style. Blend in parts of your personal life and your journey as an artist to make it more personable and relatable.

3.4. Curating Content Reflecting Your Artistic Vision

Your posts and their themes should align with your artistic vision. Share pieces of your finest work, behind-the-scenes footage, your creative process, inspirations, struggles, and achievements. Maintaining a balance between personal and professional content can offer a well-rounded glimpse into your life as an artist. Be selective and ensure the rhythm of posts matches your artistic cadence.

3.5. Amplifying Your Online Persona with a Bio

An artist's bio on social media serves two purposes: to provide an introduction to newcomers and further establish the persona for regular visitors. A good bio is succinct, engaging, informative, and flavored with your personality. Share your artistry, your vision, your achievements and spice it up with a touch of personal trivia. For instance, "Abstract painter with a penchant for bold colors. Aiming to disrupt the monotony of mundane with my art. Three-time State Art

Awardee and a dog lover."

3.6. Engaging with Your Audience

Your online presence isn't just about broadcasting your artwork; it's also about interaction. Engage with your followers by responding to their comments, messages, and shares. Show appreciation for their support and reciprocate the love and compliments. This not only fosters a sense of community but also adds depth to your persona, showcasing your amiable side.

3.7. Learning from Inspirations and Role Models

Analyzing successful artists' personas on social media can provide valuable insights and inspirations for crafting your persona. Make a note of what forms their persona, the elements of their interactions, their distinctive voice, the way they showcase their art, and how they engage with their followers.

In crafting an online persona as an artist, every detail matters and contributes to your overall image. It's an ongoing process, a journey of self-reflection, and meticulous orchestration of different elements. Though it may seem exerting and, at times, even bewildering, remember that authenticity and consistency are the key aspects. Keep true to your art and yourself, and your online persona will naturally resonate with your audience. Remember, the essence of social media is 'being social'—a genuine, transparent, and engaging persona usually works best in this cooperative space.

Chapter 4. Artistic Strategy: Tailoring Your Content to Different Platforms

In this transformatively digital time, the seed of an artist's success is firmly rooted in grasping the theoretical underpinnings of social media platforms and the strategic deployment of crafted content. As an artist, your creative output not only must be engaging but also should be platform-specific to maximize engagement and visibility. When the art world meets the digital domain, these nuances of content tailoring become vital for cracking the code of successful digital artistic presence.

4.1. Understanding Platform Specificity

The first step towards effective tailored content strategy is understanding that different social platforms cater to varied audience demographics, and their algorithms function distinctly. Hence, uniform content across all platforms may not yield the expected outcomes.

Facebook, being one of the older platforms, has a broader demographic user base that savours in-depth content. Instagram caters to a relatively younger audience, favoring visuals and brief captions. Twitter's brevity-driven culture demands concise yet impactful tweets, while LinkedIn appeals to a professional readership, preferring insightful, industry-related content. Pinterest, on the other hand, caters to an audience seeking inspiration and tends to favor infographic-style posts.

Understanding the above delineations forms the groundwork for designing tailored content, which balances platform-specific user preferences and algorithmic demands.

4.2. Tailoring Content: A Platform by Platform Guide

4.2.1. Facebook: In-Depth Narratives and Engagement

The expansive nature of Facebook equips you to share a mix of content, including photo albums, extensive write-ups, live videos, and even event announcements. The diverse range of options allows you to showcase not just the finished piece of art, but also the journey behind its creation, building a narrative that invites deeper user engagement.

An optimal Facebook post might be a photo album documenting the stages of your latest project with a detailed descriptive narrative, inviting discussion or opinions. This technique exhibits your process and invites your audience to engage, creating touchpoints that build familiarity and affinity for your art.

4.2.2. Instagram: Captivating Imagery and Hashtag Savvy

Renowned for its visual-centric interface, Instagram demands high-quality, aesthetically pleasing images. As an artist, utilize this space to give your art the spotlight drawn in the best light. Sharing snippets of your work process through Instagram Stories keeps your followers engaged and looking forward to the final piece. The use of hashtags is significant on Instagram; using targeted, relevant hashtags can extend your reach significantly.

An Instagram post might feature an HD photograph of your artwork, accompanied by a concise yet compelling caption and a curated selection of hashtags. Consider teaser posts and time-lapse videos of your artwork to boost engagement.

4.2.3. Twitter: Brevity and Timeliness

Twitter's fast-paced, character-limited environment is conducive for timely updates, sparking discussions, or sharing interesting art facts and quick thoughts. Follow the trending hashtags relevant to your field and participate in discussions to stay visible and engage with your community.

A tweet might feature a succinct insight about your creative journey or muse, an image of your art piece, or a thought-provoking question that incites dialogue within the art community.

4.2.4. LinkedIn: Industry Insights and Professional Growth

LinkedIn's professional audience appreciates insightful, meaningful content. Share your experiences at art workshops or exhibitions, industry insights, or thoughts on professional growth in the art industry.

A LinkedIn post could detail your learnings from a recent art symposium, an analytical piece on art market trends, or your art journey as a professional—accentuating your legitimacy and prompting industry networking opportunities.

4.2.5. Pinterest: Inspiration and Infographics

People often flock to Pinterest seeking inspiration. Pin beautiful, high-quality images of your artwork that might ignite an idea in a fellow artist or appeal to art enthusiasts. Infographic-style posts depicting "step-by-step creation" or "behind-the-artwork" stories are popular.

A Pinterest post might be an infographic documenting your typical day as an artist or a high-quality image of your artwork, with precise keywords for effective searchability.

4.3. Coherence in Diversity

While tailoring content to each platform's specifics, maintaining a coherent and authentic artistic voice across all platforms is crucial. This coherence bolsters your recognition as an artist and fosters trust among your audience, moulding your unique artistic identity amidst the ever-evolving digital panorama.

With keen understanding, strategic modifications and articulate execution of the principles mentioned, you're now ready to curate a bespoke social media content strategy that not only showcases your artwork but also crafts a compelling narrative around your artistic journey. Harness this knowledge and ascend to new heights in the digital art world!

Chapter 5. Understanding Social Media Algorithms: From Puzzle to Palette

Social media presents a beautiful yet bewildering convergence of art, technology, and human interaction. Behind the facades of glittering images and tittering emojis, there's a conundrum of algorithms at work. These mathematical phenomena might seem like a complicated puzzle at first glance, but they're essentially the brushes and paints you'll be using to transform your social media canvas into a vibrant masterpiece of user engagement and audience growth.

5.1. Decoding The Social Media Algorithm

To simplify, social media algorithms are sets of rules that determine what content users see on their feed. They aren't arbitrary laws, but quite specifically geared to optimize user experience. Based on users' preferences and actions, the algorithms create a customized flow that decides which posts get exposure and which are relegated to the backstage.

It's akin to a grand puppeteer orchestrating a show catered to individual's tastes. If a user frequently engages with a particular artist's content, the algorithm takes note and shows more of that artist's work. This works inversely as well; if they less frequently engage with another artist, its content gets fewer impressions on their feed.

5.2. The Role of Engagement

Engagement is the key to unlocking the algorithm's favor. It refers to likes, comments, shares, saves, and the time spent viewing a post or a story. This forms the data substrate on which the algorithm paints the user's social media narrative. Increasing your engagement metrics subsequently increases your visibility within the algorithm's framework—a performance metric every artist should consider.

5.3. 'Post' For Success – Timing And Frequency

Time your expressions for maximum engagement. Optimal posting times vary per platform and audience, but generally align with typical social media browsing habits. Imagine you've created a breathtaking sunset painting. Publishing it when your audience is most likely to be on their devices enhances your chances of capturing their attention.

Remember to saturate but not supersaturate. Posting frequently helps maintain audience interest and algorithmic visibility. But inundating feeds with posts can lead to diminished engagement rates and could even irk your followers. Strike a sustainable balance between silence and noise.

5.4. The Relevance of Content

Though it might seem like a no-brainer, the relevance of your content is crucial. You could be posting the most stunning images or writing compelling narratives, but if they're irrelevant to your art or your audience, they might not resonate.

Imagine painting vivid narratives with your artwork. If the imagery and accompanying text fail to communicate or captivate the audience's interest, algorithms will withhold that from future feeds. Hence, it's essential to use language and visuals that connect with your audience and reflect the essence of your art.

5.5. Reigning Algorithms: Facebook, Instagram, and Twitter

Understanding platform-specific algorithms is essential in tailoring your strategy. Facebook prioritizes content users engage with the most. It's a tale of relevance, engagement and recency. Instagram follows a similar pattern but also incorporates factors like relationship histories and the likelihood of the user engaging with specific content.

Twitter, on the other hand, uses a blend of algorithmic and chronological timelines. It identifies what it considers the most relevant Tweets based on the user's interactions and presents them in a section called 'Top Tweets,' while the rest remain in the 'Latest Tweets' section – more chronologically arranged.

5.6. Conclusion: The Palette of Opportunity

As enigmatic as they may appear initially, social media algorithms present artists with an invaluable palette of opportunities. To master them, you must first understand them. Just as each canvas poses its unique challenges and opportunities, so does each social media algorithm. The complicated puzzle gradually transforms into a palette – an array of opportunities to create your unique brand, engage your audience, and bring your art to the world.

Success in the social media sphere isn't purely about creating great art. It's about using the algorithms strategically, just as you employ specific strokes, colors and effects in your artwork. Harness these digital tools effectively, and you're halfway towards designing your masterpiece of popularity, growth and influence on social media. Unravel these complexities, and the social media canvas is all yours to paint.

Chapter 6. Telling Your Story: The Art of Social Media Copywriting

Storytelling is, and always has been, a cornerstone of human connection. As an artist, your art already tells a story. How we illuminate that story on social media can make all the difference to your reception and reach. This chapter aims to guide you to elegantly express your narrative through social media copywriting.

6.1. What is Social Media Copywriting?

Social media copywriting is merely a fancy term for the art of writing text for your social media posts. It's the catchphrase under that beautiful painting, the delicate prose describing your latest sculpture, the intriguing mysteries whispered beneath your graphic designs. It's stringing words together to catch attention, invoke emotions, spark curiosity, or nudge your followers to take desired actions. In essence, it's your written voice and it contributes significantly to your online persona.

6.2. The Impact of Copywriting on Engagement

At its core, social media is about socialization. Good copywriting can transform your social media profiles from mere art showcases to engaging platforms for dialogue and interaction. It prompts readers to comment, like or share, increasing the post's virality and extending your reach. Well-crafted copy can make your fans feel connected to you, melding your art and your audience in ways never before possible.

6.3. Elements of Compelling Copywriting

There are four essential elements that contribute to effective social media copywriting: clarity, brevity, relevance, and value. Clarity refers to the capacity to convey your message in the most understandable way. Brevity, on the other hand, is about making an impact in as few words as possible—remember, this is social media, not a novel! Relevance means ensuring your content resonates with your audience. Finally, adding value means there should be a takeaway, be it information, inspiration, motivation, or entertainment.

6.4. Creating a Unified Brand Voice

An artist's brand voice, like art, is unique. Just as your art style sets you apart, so should your writing. This voice infuses your personality into your words, forming a connection with the audience. It should be consistent across all social media platforms, making you instantly recognizable. Think about your artistic style, your values, your purpose—allow these to shape your brand voice.

6.5. Storytelling Through Copywriting

In a sea of content, what makes your art stand out is its story. Tell the story behind your creation, the challenges you faced, what inspired you. Were you charmed by a sunset, moved to tears by a book, stirred by a melody? Share your journey. This imbues your artworks with added depth and magnetism. Use strong, appropriate verbs and adjectives to evoke the emotions you felt during the creation process.

Your followers aren't just buying your art, they're buying the fascinating journey that led to it.

6.6. Crafting Calls to Action

As an artist, it's not enough to simply post and hope for the best. Each post should have a purpose beyond sharing—but to connect, engage, inform, entertain, or even sell. A clear call to action (CTA) guides your audience on the next step. Whether that's to check out your latest blog, visit an exhibition, purchase a print or simply express their thoughts in the comments, your CTA turns passive viewers into active participants in your artistic journey.

6.7. Understanding Hashtags and SEO

In social media, hashtags are like breadcrumb trails leading potential followers to your posts. Understanding hashtag and SEO mechanics add visibility to your posts, improve your presence and increase your art's discoverability. Leveraging popular and relevant hashtags in your copy ensures your work surfaces in searches and conversations about those particular themes and topics.

6.8. Practicing and refining your social media copywriting

Just like perfecting an art form, enhancing your copywriting skills takes time. Practice is key. Experiment with different writing styles and formats. Monitor which ones resonate the most with your audience. Learn from your successes and failures. Similarly like creating art, copywriting is an iterative process.

Copywriting is an extended brush in your creative toolbox, allowing you to paint richer, deeper layers onto the canvas of your artwork's story. By understanding and applying these principles, you can shape your artistic narrative in compelling ways. This could be the difference between being just another artist or a memorable storyteller in the social media realm. As an artist, you have a story to tell. Let's ensure it's heard.

Chapter 7. Hashtags & Strategies: Targeting the Right Audience

Hashtags provide a linchpin for artists on social media platforms to connect their works with relevant digital communities. When employed strategically, these pertinent strings of characters can transform posts into tuned signals, emitting your art across the vast digital universe. Therefore, the cornerstone of any social media strategy that aims to land your art in the right audience's feed should be understanding and exploiting the power of hashtags.

7.1. Understanding the Power of Hashtags

The first key step to appreciating hashtags' significance is understanding the mechanism behind them. At a basic level, hashtags - denoted by a pound symbol (#) followed by a string of text - serve two primary functions: They categorize content, and they create a digital communication trail. And for artists, they also serve a third function: They can act as searchable keywords, enabling users interested in specific types of art to easily locate your posts.

When you use a hashtag, social media platforms automatically index the post, making it discoverable to everyone searching for that hashtag. A well-chosen hashtag can lead the right audience to your doorstep—the viewers actively seeking the artistic experience that your work delivers.

7.2. Pay Attention to Relevant Hashtags in Your Niche

Every artist, irrespective of their form and style, resides within a specific niche or several in the vast art ecosystem. Identifying the relevant hashtags within your niche(s) is crucial in effectively positioning your content for the right audience.

Start by deep diving into your artistic genre. Whether you excel in abstract painting, digital art, pottery, or sculpture, begin by tracking the hashtags commonly used by artists operating within the same genre. Experiment with different keyword combinations, such as #AbstractArt, #DigitalArtists, or #PotteryLove. See how different variations, like #SculptorLife or #LifeOfASculptor, affect your post reach. This process will allow you to refine your hashtag strategy and discover the keywords your target audience frequently uses when searching for art.

7.3. The Balanced Use of Broad and Specific Hashtags

Avoiding the extremes of using overly broad or overly specific hashtags is a salient aspect of hashtag strategy. Broad hashtags like #Art or #Artist cater to a wide user network but can risk submerging your posts in a sea of countless others, diluting your visibility. Specific tags, conversely, offer a more targeted approach, allowing you to connect with precise communities of interest.

A balanced mix of parity is key: blend general, community-specific, and personalized hashtags to maximize your reach. For instance, an abstract artist could use a combination of #Art (broad), #AbstractArt (niche-specific), and #YourNameAbstract (personalized).

7.4. Hashtag Research and Trending Topics

The use of trending hashtags offers another method of extending your post reach. By engaging with trending conversations relevant to your realm, you're more likely to increase your visibility and attract the right audience. Follow popular art pages, influencers, and art communities on your chosen social media platforms. Keep a pulse on how they use hashtags, the ones that generate most interactions, and any shift in conversation trends.

Also, invest time in researching the suggested hashtags on different social platforms—Instagram and LinkedIn, for instance, offer a list of related hashtags once you start typing it in the post section.

7.5. Hashtag Limit and Over-Hashtagging

Platforms have different rules around how many hashtags you can use. Instagram allows up to 30, Twitter encourages no more than 2, while LinkedIn recommends no more than 5. Respecting these limits and avoiding 'hashtag stuffing' (adding excess hashtags without real context or value) keeps your posts aesthetically pleasing and functional.

Remember, the goal of using hashtags is to make your content accessible to your target audience while keeping posts neat and easy to engage with—creating a balance between these two is crucial in targeting the right audience with your art.

7.6. Leveraging Hashtags: Developing Your Unique Voice

Lastly, make sure to align your hashtag use with your brand's voice. Custom hashtags like your artist name, art series, or even specially designed campaigns can drive more attention to your work, creating a stronger brand identity and a sense of community among your followers. For example, if you're launching a digital art series, think about encapsulating the series in a unique hashtag, #DigitalArtSeriesByYourName.

Remember, the art of mastering hashtags lies in continuous testing and refinement of your strategy, just like art itself. It requires experimenting with different compositions, learning from your engagements, and understanding trends. Thus, much like creating a sensational art piece, creating the perfect hashtag strategy is no different—it's an art in itself.

Armed with a meticulously chosen arsenal of hashtags and a tenacious spirit of experimentation, you're well on your way to painting a beautiful masterpiece on the broad canvas of social media, reaching the discerning eyes of your perfect audience. Dive into this newfound world and witness your art be discovered, appreciated, and loved.

Chapter 8. Engaging Your Followers: Building Community Through Interaction

Social media is a grand stage, a debate forum, a confession booth, and a classroom, conceivably, all rolled into one. It has evolved to house a bustling agora where artists, just like you, paint with stories, brush with creative ideas, and frame the ordinary in an extraordinary light. You may have mastered the art of leveraging hashtags, tailored your content to the tastes of various platforms, and comprehended the algorithms to a satisfactory degree. But all these learned skills pale without an essential element, which is audience engagement. This vital chapter underscores the value of proactively fostering connections and building a community through thoughtful interaction with your followers.

8.1. The Essence of Interaction

In the vast world of the internet, interaction and engagement are key. This is particularly potent for artists. Social media, in essence, acts as a two-way communication channel where you aren't just showcasing your artwork but also engaging in meaningful dialogue. Nurturing rich connections with your followers will grant you a responsive audience that is enthralled by your work and invested in your artistic journey.

Engagement is more than just a simple like, share, or comment. It's about making your followers feel valued, seen, and acknowledged. Showcase your authenticity by aligning your online persona with your true self. Respond to comments, thank your followers for their support, or even ask for their opinions on your upcoming projects. A simple act like mentioning a follower in a post can go a long way in building a bond.

8.2. Personalizing Your Approach

Every follower is a potential ambassador of your art, an influencer on a micro-level, sharing your work with their circles, thereby expanding your reach. Yet, she or he is more than just a number incrementing your follower count. Behind every profile picture, there lies an individual with distinct tastes, perspectives, and inspirations. To develop a rapport with them, it is essential to tailor your interactions, considering the diversity among your followers.

It could involve sending personalized direct messages, altering your language style to match your fan base, or sharing content that resonates with them. Provide glimpses into your creative processes, share 'behind-the-scene' snippets, or organize regular Q&A sessions. Gradually, these actions will reduce the gap between you and your followers, forging a robust community around your art.

8.3. Influencing with Content

As cliched as it might sound, content indeed is king. What you share on your social media channels influences how your followers perceive you and your work. Engaging content will incite interest, conversation, and emotions among your followers.

Producing diverse content is also effective – from in-depth blog posts about your workflow to shorter, more digestible infographics about your upcoming exhibitions. Variety ensures the sustained attention of your followers, thereby multiplying interactions. Consider employing interactive content types like polls, quizzes, or contests—which are not only fun but also handy tools to gather follower opinions.

8.4. Driven by Data

Data is a treasure trove for those wishing to optimize their social media engagement. Platforms like Instagram, Facebook, Twitter, etc., have built-in analytical tools that offer insights into your audience's behavior. Review these metrics to understand what works and what doesn't. For example, ascertain the type of content that resonates with your followers, optimal posting times, or user demographics. These insights can guide your engagement strategy, enabling you to cater better to your audience.

8.5. Cultivating Community Feel

Evolve from being a solitary artist to the leader of an artistically inclined community. This step will involve spotlighting follower artworks, holding collaborative projects, or even hosting online art challenges. Offering such platforms not only cells to foster unity among your followers but empowers them to engage more personally with your content.

The road to building a thriving social media community is iterative. It demands patience, consistency, and adaptability. Yet, it holds within it the potential to transform your journey, turning your passion into a shared experience. As you let your art transcend borders and cultures, remember that in this digital age, art is no longer confined to canvas. It's a dialogue—an interaction—that holds within it the power to inspire, connect, and influence. And you, dear artist, are the spark that keeps this conversation ablaze.

Chapter 9. Leveraging Influencers and Collaborations in Your Field

In the contemporary digital world, collaborations and partnerships with influencers have become key strategies for broadening your audience and enhancing your online visibility. This chapter will provide an exhaustive guide on how artists can purposefully and effectively leverage influencers and collaborations in their field.

9.1. Understanding Influencer Marketing

Influencer marketing isn't a novel concept but a newly digitalized and reinvented version of an old marketing formula: getting a popular individual to vouch for your product. The rise of social media has revolutionized the way this conventional marketing technique operates. Influencers are social media users who have established credibility in a specific industry and have a large audience that they can persuade by virtue of their authenticity and reach.

When an artist collaborates with an influencer, their art might be featured in a post, reviewed, or recommended on a blog, Instagram story, Facebook post, or tweet. This type of promotion can swiftly expand an artist's reach, sometimes overnight, exposing their work to a fresh and engaged audience.

9.2. Identifying the Right Influencers

Identifying the right influencers for your art requires careful considerations and a deep understanding of your art form, your target audience, and the influencer's field of interest. Artists should aim to collaborate with influencers who authentically align with their art form and style. Relevance, authenticity, engagement rates, and audience demographics should be considered when identifying an apt influencer.

It's essential to do some research: - Look for influencers whose art style, aesthetic, or interests align with yours. - Analyze their audience demographics to see if they match your target audience. - Assess how active they are and the engagement quality on their profile to ascertain their influence.

9.3. Collaborating With Influencers

Once you've identified influencers that you'd like to collaborate with, the next step is to pitch your proposal. Be genuine, concise, and clear about what the collaboration could look like and what both parties would gain from it. Collaborations could include: - Joint art projects or competitions - Guest posts or takeovers on each other's platforms - Product reviews or feature posts - Virtual artist meets or Q&A sessions

Remember, the symbiotic nature of the collaboration is crucial. Even though the artist might obtain visibility and audience from the influencer, make sure to offer something of equal value in return.

9.4. Harnessing the Power of Collaborations

Beyond influencers, collaborations with peers or related brands in your field can provide reciprocal benefits. Collaborating with other artists or brands can often increase exposure for both parties involved, either by sharing audiences or by creating something entirely new and exciting that captures the attention of a larger collective audience.

When collaborating, consider the following: - Create co-branded content or projects that reflect both artists' inputs. - Host virtual art exhibitions or open houses together. - Collaborate on unique collections that combine the unique stylistic elements of each artist. - Jointly conduct workshops or masterclasses.

These collaborative attempts amplify the reach of your art and open up new avenues and opportunities you may not have considered previously.

9.5. Analyzing Success and Measuring Impact

The last part of utilizing influencers and collaborations to your advantage is the critical task of analyzing success and measuring impact. Social media platforms offer various analytical tools to track the extent of the reach, interaction, and engagement of your collaborative posts. Pay close attention to changes in follower count, engagement rate, and content interactions.

Remember that the measure of success should be in alignment with your goals. If the aim of the collaboration was to increase followers, then a surge of new follower counts is a success. If the goal was enhancing your reach, then impressions and engagement rates would be excellent indicators of success.

In conclusion, the strategic use of influencer marketing and collaborations can serve as a potent tool for artists in the social media space. With a well-thought-out strategy, the right influencers, and purposeful collaborations, artists can give their work the digital wings to fly across the diverse social media landscape. The artists who navigate this terrain with the percipience can carve out a distinctive online identity for their art and can maximize the rewards from the burgeoning digital artistry market. Finally, always remember to maintain authenticity and personal connection with your digital audience because, at the heart of it, art is a universal language of human connection.

Chapter 10. Case Studies: Analyzing Successful Artists on Social Media

The realm of social media has been transformed into a canvas where artists are not simply pushing their creative boundaries, but also establishing a platform that allows them to gain maximum recognition and reach the heart of art lovers, far and wide. In this chapter, we will unpack various case studies that focus on successful artists who have harnessed the potential of social media for the expansion and growth of their artistic endeavors.

10.1. Embracing Instagram: The Case of Ashley Longshore

Our first study focuses on the eccentric and exuberant mixed-media artist, Ashley Longshore, who has magnificently tamed Instagram for her artistic goals. Based in New Orleans, Longshore's daring humor brings a distinctive flavor to her art that could be best described as pop-art with a witty twist. With over 479,000 followers, Longshore's success was not an overnight process but a visceral and raw journey infused with her strong personality.

Primarily, Longshore offered viewers candid behind-the-scenes glimpses into her vibrant life and artistic process. She let her followers peek into the 'why' and 'how' of her creations, building an intimate space where people personally connected with her and her artwork. She developed an authentic voice, leveraging her southern charm and wit, often accompanied by bold statements against societal norms and cultural tropes. Her posts were her palette, blending the colors of her life with those of her artistry. This openness, teamed with her brilliant artistic talent, has set her apart from the crowd, further magnifying the appeal that has drawn a massive Instagram following.

10.2. Breaking Boundaries on Twitter: David Shrigley

The British artist David Shrigley, renowned for his whimsical and slightly macabre illustrations, escalated the utilization of Twitter to a whole new level. With nearly 244,000 followers, Shrigley's approach to the social media platform was one part casual conversation, one part eccentric artistic showcase, resulting in an interactive digital art space.

Shrigley's Twitter success is largely attributable to his ability to integrate his peculiar art style into a seemingly casual conversation with his followers. He uses the platform to share glimpses of his works-in-progress, engage in everyday chatter, and drop absurdly funny tidbits that reflect his unique artistic sense. He indulges creatively with the platform, playing with its format to yield an amalgamation of his art and text, fueled by his distinctively quirky sense of humor. This engaging playfulness has aided in creating an active rapport with his followers, thus amplifying his visibility and reach on Twitter.

10.3. Digital Domination on TikTok: Sarah Perez

One cannot ignore the wave of the digital art scene that has swept the social media world, especially on TikTok, where millions of people share their personal and artistic journeys in brief video clips. Sarah Perez, a young digital artist famously known for her viral video transformations, is a trailblazer in the TikTok creative community.

Possessing over 1.3 million followers, Perez saw the potential of

TikTok as a platform not merely for displaying her skill but for communicating the process of her creation, thereby breathing life into her artworks. She shares timelapse videos of her digital art creations, providing her followers with a mesmerizing view of her work being born on-screen. By drawing viewers into her creative journey, she forms a deep connection with her audience. Furthermore, she frequently engages with her followers, responding to comments, fulfilling art-related requests, and sharing tips. Her rigorous and robust interaction has helped her art reach going viral repeatedly on TikTok.

In conclusion, each platform has its unique strengths, challenges, and user culture, and understanding these enable artists to harness them to their advantage. These case studies offer a peek into successful personalized strategies. However, it's vital to realize that each artist's journey is unique, and what works for one might not necessarily work for others. The most potent strategy in the world of social media is remaining authentic, consistent, and keeping the communication channels open with your audience. Therefore, it is incumbent upon the artist to invest time in understanding the platform chosen, meshing its strengths with their unique style, mastering their messaging, and evolving their strategies through trial-and-error, as the digital sphere evolves.

Chapter 11. Looking Ahead: Future Trends in Social Media for Artists

As we find ourselves on the brink of the unknown, it's important to understand that the world of social media is not static. It's an ever-evolving entity that reshapes itself with every trend, every click, every hashtag, and every comment. The undercurrents of change run deep and wide, bringing artists closer to a global audience like never before. Let's observe the horizon of this digital landscape and envisage the upcoming trends in social media for artists.

11.1. The Rise of Short-Form Videos

In the realm of social media promotion, the charm of short-form video content continues to manifest its ubiquity with leapfrogging popularity. Platforms like TikTok, Instagram Reels, and YouTube Shorts have dominated the scene, immortalising this format. As an artist, harnessing the power of this compact, easily digestible content can create an intimate bond with your audience as they take a deep dive into your creative process with quick snippets. You can use these videos to bring your art to life, illustrate your artistic process, host brisk tutorials, create time-lapse content of your work, or even discuss the themes and thought processes behind your creations.

11.2. Augmented Reality and Virtual Reality

Next on the horizon are Augmented Reality (AR) and Virtual Reality (VR). These immersive technologies have completely altered the ways we experience art, transcending the two-dimensional screen.

Instagram and Snapchat's AR filters are just the tip of the iceberg—expect to see newer, more sophisticated applications of AR and VR technology in the art sphere. For instance, VR could enable artists to host virtual gallery exhibitions, while AR could be used to project artwork in various physical settings, offering audiences a unique and tailored viewing experience.

11.3. Growing Importance of Algorithm Literacy

Algorithm literacy or understanding the decryption of ever-evolving sets of coded social media rules is a burgeoning necessity for artists who wish to stay at the top of their game. The digital algorithms dictate the visibility and reach of your posts, and hence, grasping their workings is critical. Expect future social media platforms to design more transparent algorithms, giving users greater insight into how their content is distributed and to whom. In alignment with this shift, artists must consistently educate themselves about these algorithmic shifts to craft their online presence more effectively.

11.4. Rise of Social Commerce

Artists can look forward to an increased focus on social commerce—a seamless integration of shopping experiences into social media platforms. Understanding and leveraging social commerce can lead to increased sales of your artwork, prints, and merchandise directly via social media, thereby reducing the dependency on galleries or third-party websites. Platforms such as Instagram and Facebook have already introduced integrated shopping features, allowing artists to set up virtual storefronts to exhibit and sell their work.

11.5. Emphasizing Authenticity and Storytelling

In the future, merely showcasing artwork won't be sufficient. The audience craves connection—a deeper understanding of the artist and the story behind their creations. An engaging narrative about your artistic journey, your inspiration, and challenges can make your work more relatable and appealing, fostering a stronger emotional connection with your followers. Interactive elements and direct communication tools like Q&As, live videos, and personal anecdotes will likely play an even bigger role in promoting this sense of connection.

11.6. Utilization of Big Data and Analytics

The expansive rise of Big Data and analytics can provide artists with insightful details about their audience's behaviour, preferences, and engagement patterns. Reliable data can help tailor content strategies, improve audience targeting, streamline promotional efforts, and enhance engagement. Artists who understand the value of data-driven decisions will find it easier to connect with potential followers, buyers, and collaborators, translating into more effective social media usage.

11.7. Thriving on User-Generated Content

User-Generated Content (UGC) augments the cultivation of a community around your art. Expect to see more artists inviting their followers to participate in challenges, share user-made art based on your tutorials, or create content that directly engages with your work. UGC not only strengthens your brand through validation but also diversifies your content and enhances your reach through follower networks.

Understanding and embracing these trends are crucial. It's evident that navigating the future of social media for artists will entail more than just displaying artwork—it will involve telling captivating stories, engaging with audiences on a personal level, understanding the underlying mechanics of platforms, leveraging emerging technologies, and building a powerful, resonant digital brand. It's an exciting journey, where your canvas goes beyond the physical world, entering the dynamic arena of the online space, where new artistic narratives will unfold. Be ready; this fascinating new epoch embraces every artist willing to surf the digital wave.